Contents

What's Great About This Book

Centers are a wonderful, fun way for students to practice important skills. The 13 centers in this book are self-contained and portable. Students may work at a desk, at a table, or even on the floor. Once you've made the centers, they're ready to use any time.

What's in This Book

The teacher directions page includes how to make the center and a description of the student task

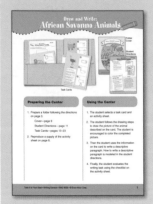

Full-color materials needed for the center

Reproducible activity sheets to practice and evaluate writing skills

Portfolio cover and a student center checklist

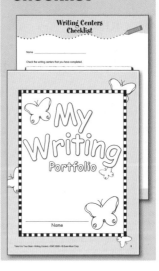

How to Use the Centers

The centers are intended for skill practice, not to introduce skills. It is important to model the use of each center before students do the task independently.

Questions to Consider:

- Will students select a center, or will you assign the centers?
- Will there be a specific block of time for centers, or will the centers be used throughout the day?
- Where will you place the centers for easy access by students?
- What procedure will students use when they need help with the center tasks?
- How will you track the tasks and centers completed by each student?

Making a File Folder Center

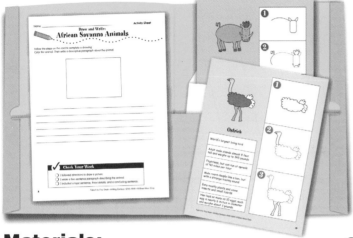

Folder centers are easily stored in a box or file crate. Students take a folder to their desks to complete the task.

Materials:

- folder with pockets
- envelopes
- marking pens and pencils
- scissors
- stapler
- two-sided tape

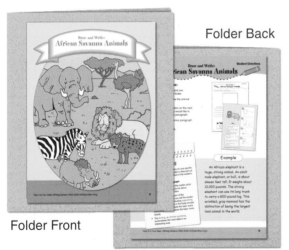

Folder Back

Folder Front

Steps to Follow:

1. Laminate the cover. Tape it to the front of the folder.

2. Laminate the student directions page. Tape it to the back of the folder.

3. Place activity sheets, writing paper, and any other supplies in the left-hand pocket.

4. Laminate the task cards. Place each set of task cards in an envelope. Place the labeled envelopes in the right-hand pocket.

5. If needed for the center, laminate the sorting mat and place it in the right-hand pocket of the folder.

6. If needed for the center, laminate and assemble the self-checking answer key pages into a booklet. Place them in the left-hand pocket of the folder.

Student Portfolio

If desired, make a writing portfolio for each student. Reproduce pages 5 and 6 for each student. Attach the cover to the front of a file folder. Attach the student center checklist to the inside front cover of the folder. Place the portfolio folders in an area accessible to both students and teacher.

Center Checklist

Student Names

Centers

Centers												
Draw and Write: African Savanna Animals												
Idioms												
The Best and the Worst												
Synonym Power												
Poetry Works												
In the News												
Fun Fables												
Letter to the Editor												
Comic Strips												
Plan a Story												
A Personal Narrative												
Tongue Twisters												
Editing Workshop												

Take It to Your Seat—Writing Centers • EMC 6006 • © Evan-Moor Corp.

My Writing
Portfolio

_____
Name

Writing Centers Checklist

Name _____

Check the writing centers that you have completed.

❑ Draw and Write: African Savanna Animals

❑ Idioms

❑ The Best and the Worst

❑ Synonym Power

❑ Poetry Works

❑ In the News

❑ Fun Fables

❑ Letter to the Editor

❑ Comic Strips

❑ Plan a Story

❑ A Personal Narrative

❑ Tongue Twisters

❑ Editing Workshop

Draw and Write:
African Savanna Animals

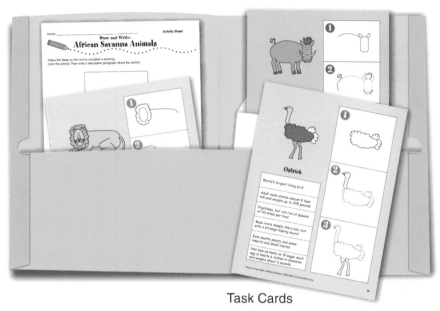

Task Cards

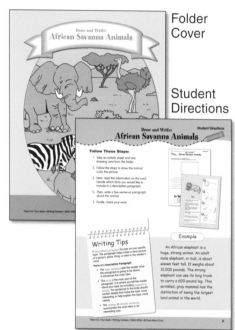

Folder Cover

Student Directions

Preparing the Center

1. Prepare a folder following the directions on page 3.

   Cover—page 9

   Student Directions—page 11

   Task Cards—pages 13–23

2. Reproduce a supply of the activity sheet on page 8.

Using the Center

1. The student selects a task card and an activity sheet.

2. The student follows the drawing steps to draw the picture of the animal described on the card. The student is encouraged to color the completed picture.

3. Then the student uses the information on the card to write a descriptive paragraph. How to write a descriptive paragraph is modeled in the student directions.

4. Finally, the student evaluates the writing task using the checklist on the activity sheet.

Draw and Write:
African Savanna Animals

Follow the steps on the card to complete a drawing.
Color the animal. Then write a descriptive paragraph about the animal.

_____

_____

_____

_____

_____

✔ Check Your Work

○ I followed directions to draw a picture.

○ I wrote a five-sentence paragraph describing the animal.

○ I included a topic sentence, three details, and a concluding sentence.

Draw and Write:
African Savanna Animals

Draw and Write:
African Savanna Animals

Follow These Steps:

1. Take an activity sheet and one drawing card from the folder.

2. Follow the steps to draw the animal. Color the picture.

3. Next, read the information on the card. Decide which facts you would like to include in a descriptive paragraph.

4. Then, write a five-sentence paragraph about the animal.

5. Finally, check your work.

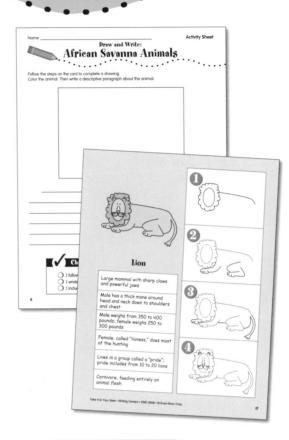

Writing Tips

A descriptive paragraph focuses on one specific topic. The paragraph helps make a clear picture of a person, place, thing, or idea in the reader's mind.

Parts of a Descriptive Paragraph

- The topic sentence tells the reader what the paragraph is going to be about. It introduces the main idea.

- The body is the main part of the paragraph. It is where you tell the reader about your topic by including supporting details. The sentences in the body should contain details that make the topic more interesting or help explain the topic more clearly.

- The closing, or clincher sentence, summarizes the main idea in an interesting way.

Example

An African elephant is a huge, strong animal. An adult male elephant, or bull, is about eleven feet tall. It weighs about 12,000 pounds. The strong elephant can use its long trunk to carry a 600-pound log. This wrinkled, gray mammal has the distinction of being the largest land animal in the world.

Elephant

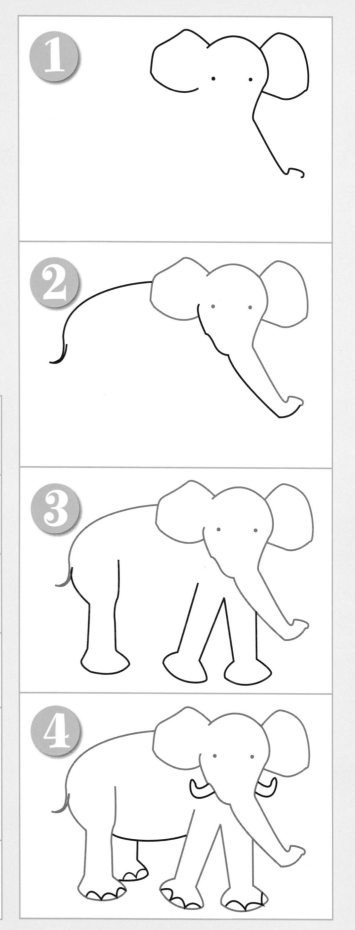

Wrinkled-skinned gray mammal is largest land animal
Adult male (bull) is about 11 feet tall; weighs about 12,000 pounds
Uses trunk as a hand; trunk can carry a 600-pound log or an object as small as a coin
Two ivory tusks are really long, curved upper teeth
Females (cows) and their young (calves) live in families of about 10 members; family unit led by the oldest female, called a "matriarch"
Herbivore; eats grass, water plants, and all parts of trees

Draw and Write:
African Savanna Animals

© Evan-Moor Corp. • EMC 6006

Spotted Hyena

Mammal famous for its howl, which sounds like a hysterical human laugh
Females larger than males; about 45 inches long; weighs from 80 to 190 pounds
Powerful jaws and sharp teeth
Up to 80 live together in a large group called a "clan"
Carnivore; hunts animals such as wildebeests, zebras, and gazelles
Also a scavenger, eating dead animals

Draw and Write:
African Savanna Animals

© Evan-Moor Corp. • EMC 6006

Lion

Large mammal with sharp claws and powerful jaws
Male has a thick mane around head and neck down to shoulders and chest
Male weighs from 350 to 400 pounds; female weighs 250 to 300 pounds
Female, called "lioness," does most of the hunting
Lives in a group called a "pride"; pride includes from 10 to 20 lions
Carnivore, feeding entirely on animal flesh

Draw and Write:
African Savanna Animals

© Evan-Moor Corp. • EMC 6006

Ostrich

World's largest living bird
Adult male stands almost 8 feet tall and weighs up to 345 pounds
Flightless, but can run at speeds of 40 miles per hour
Male roars deeply like a lion, but with a strange hissing sound
Eats mostly plants and some insects and small lizards
Hen lays as many as 10 eggs; each egg is nearly 6 inches in diameter and weighs about 3 pounds

Draw and Write:
African Savanna Animals

© Evan-Moor Corp. • EMC 6006

Wart Hog

African pig with large curved tusks
Tusks about 2 feet long; also has large canine teeth
Between tusks and eyes are three pairs of large "warts"
Male (boar) weighs over 200 pounds and is about 30 inches high at shoulder
Can run up to 30 miles per hour
Eats roots, plants, birds' eggs, and small mammals

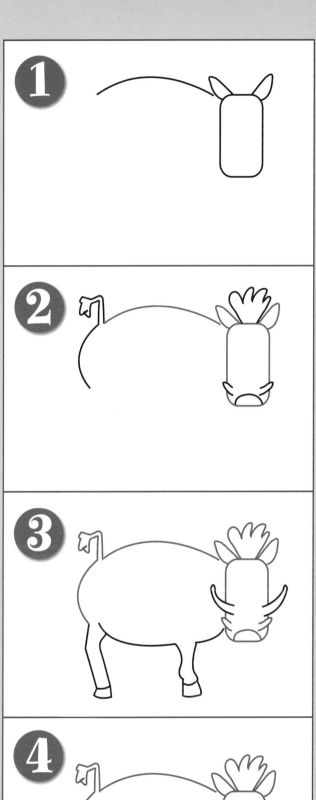

Draw and Write:
African Savanna Animals

Zebra

Striped member of horse family
No individual zebra's stripes are identical to another zebra's
Adult is over 4 feet tall and weighs about 600 pounds
Can run up to 40 miles per hour
Live in herds from a few to several hundred
Herbivore; eats grass, bark, leaves, buds, fruits, and roots

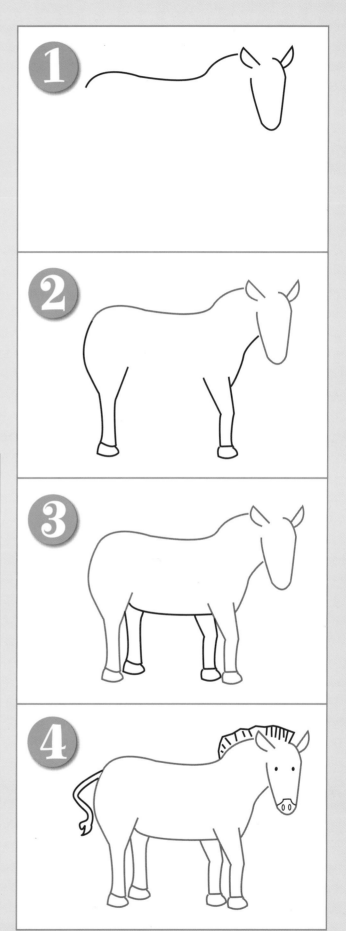

Draw and Write:
African Savanna Animals

© Evan-Moor Corp. • EMC 6006

Idioms

Puzzle Pieces

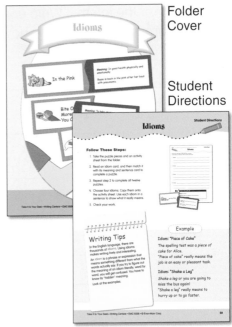

Folder Cover

Student Directions

Preparing the Center

1. Prepare a folder following the directions on page 3.

    Cover—page 27

    Student Directions—page 29

    Puzzle Pieces—pages 31–37

2. Reproduce a supply of the activity sheet on page 26.

Using the Center

1. The student takes the puzzle pieces and an activity sheet.

2. The student reads the idiom and matches it to its meaning and usage sentence to complete a puzzle. How to read and understand idioms is modeled in the student directions.

3. Next, the student repeats the steps to complete all twelve puzzles.

4. Then the student selects four idioms, writes them on the activity sheet, and uses each in a sentence to show an understanding of its meaning.

5. Finally, the student evaluates the writing task using the checklist on the activity sheet.

Name _____

Idioms

Choose four of the idioms. Write each idiom on the line.
Use the idioms in sentences to show what they *really* mean.

1. Idiom: _____

_____

_____

2. Idiom: _____

_____

_____

3. Idiom: _____

_____

_____

4. Idiom: _____

_____

_____

 ✔ Check Your Work

◯ I copied four idioms.

◯ I used each idiom in a sentence to show its meaning.

◯ I wrote complete sentences.

Idioms

In the Pink

Meaning: In good health physically and emotionally

Rosie is back *in the pink* after her bout with pneumonia.

Bite O... More ... You Ca...

Meaning: To take on more responsibilities than you can handle

Did you *bite off* ... chew... ...an ...ee

Butterfli... My Sto...

Idioms

Follow These Steps:

1. Take the puzzle pieces and an activity sheet from the folder.

2. Read an idiom card, and then match it with its meaning and sentence card to complete a puzzle.

3. Repeat step 2 to complete all twelve puzzles.

4. Choose four idioms. Copy them onto the activity sheet. Use each idiom in a sentence to show what it *really* means.

5. Check your work.

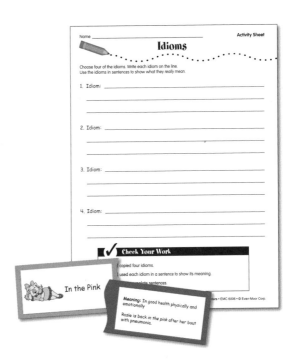

Writing Tips

In the English language, there are thousands of idioms. Using idioms makes writing lively and interesting.

An idiom is a phrase or expression that means something different from what the words actually say. If you try to figure out the meaning of an idiom literally, word by word, you will get confused. You have to know its "hidden" meaning.

Look at the examples.

Example

Idiom: "Piece of Cake"

The spelling test was a *piece of cake* for Alice.
"Piece of cake" really means the job is an easy or pleasant task.

Idiom: "Shake a Leg"

Shake a leg or you are going to miss the bus again!
"Shake a leg" really means to hurry up or to go faster.

Meaning: Awkward and clumsy, especially with the hands

Mark is unable to play really fast because he is *all thumbs*.

Meaning: Good luck; do a great job in a performance

On the night of the play, Jamie told Liliana to *break a leg*.

Meaning: To ignore danger by pretending you don't see it; to hide from obvious signs of danger

You *bury your head in the sand* if you think that smoking isn't bad for your health.

All Thumbs

Break a Leg

Bury Your Head in the Sand

Idioms

Idioms

Idioms

Idioms

Idioms

Idioms

Meaning: A fluttery feeling in the stomach caused by nervousness

I can't sing a solo without getting *butterflies in my stomach.*

Meaning: To take on more responsibilities than you can handle

Did you *bite off more than you can chew* when you agreed to work three jobs?

Meaning: In good health physically and emotionally

Rosie is back *in the pink* after her bout with pneumonia.

Butterflies in My Stomach

Bite Off More Than You Can Chew

In the Pink

Idioms

Idioms

Idioms

Idioms

Idioms

Idioms

Meaning: Identical; alike in looks and behavior

Kendra and her best friend Kirsten are *like two peas in a pod.*

Meaning: Feeling extremely happy

When Roberto won the geography bee contest, he was *on top of the world.*

Meaning: To agree fully; to have the same opinion

Natalie and Sophia *see eye to eye* about the need for bigger allowances.

Like Two
Peas in a Pod

On Top of
the World

See Eye
to Eye

Idioms

Idioms

Idioms

Idioms

Idioms

Idioms

Meaning: To tell a secret to someone who is not supposed to know it

Don't *spill the beans*, but tomorrow Mrs. Johnson is going to announce that you are our new class president.

Meaning: To act bravely in a difficult situation; to face up to a hard challenge by taking action

Take the bull by the horns and tell your neighbor that it was you that threw the ball through his window.

Meaning: To fool or trick someone

Thomas tried to *pull the wool over your eyes* when he told you that his dog ate his homework.

Spill the Beans

Take the Bull by the Horns

Pull the Wool Over Your Eyes

Idioms

© Evan-Moor Corp. • EMC 6006

Idioms

© Evan-Moor Corp. • EMC 6006

Idioms

© Evan-Moor Corp. • EMC 6006

Idioms

© Evan-Moor Corp. • EMC 6006

Idioms

© Evan-Moor Corp. • EMC 6006

Idioms

© Evan-Moor Corp. • EMC 6006

The Best and the Worst

Task Cards

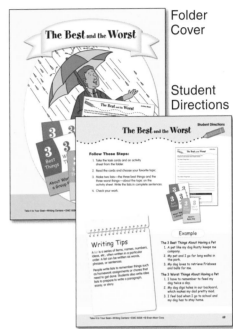

Folder Cover

Student Directions

Preparing the Center

1. Prepare a folder following the directions on page 3.

     Cover—page 41

     Student Directions—page 43

     Task Cards—pages 45–49

2. Reproduce a supply of the activity sheet on page 40.

Using the Center

1. The student takes the task cards and an activity sheet.

2. Then the student reads the cards and selects his or her favorite.

3. Next, the student writes the three best things and the three worst things about the topic. The student should write the lists in complete sentences. How to write a list is modeled in the student directions.

4. Finally, the student evaluates the writing task using the checklist on the activity sheet.
   Note: As an extension activity, the teacher may choose to have the student write a persuasive paragraph or essay using the ideas from the lists.

Name _____

The Best and the Worst

Write a list of the 3 best and the 3 worst things about the chosen topic.
The ideas for your lists should be written in complete sentences.

The 3 Best Things About _____

1. _____
   _____

2. _____
   _____

3. _____
   _____

The 3 Worst Things About _____

1. _____
   _____

2. _____
   _____

3. _____
   _____

✔ **Check Your Work**

○ I wrote the three best things about the topic.

○ I wrote the three worst things about the topic.

○ I wrote complete sentences.

The Best and the Worst

Name _____

The Best and the Worst

Write a list of the 3 best and the 3 worst things about the chosen topic. The ideas for your lists should be written in complete sentences.

The 3 Best Things About a Rainy Day

1. The sound of falling rain is relaxing to me.

2. I can curl up with a good book and read for hours.

3. On a rainy day, my dad helps me build things in the garage.

3 Worst Things About a Rainy Day

_____ y mom makes me clean my room.

_____ to the park.

_____ take the dog out for a walk.

_____ York

_____gs about the topic.

_____gs about the topic.

3
Best
Things
About Wor___
a Group P___

3
W___
T___

3
Best
Things
3
Worst
Things
About a
Rainy Day

Take It to Your Seat—Writing Centers • EMC 6006 • © Evan-Moor Corp.

The Best and the Worst

Follow These Steps:

1. Take the task cards and an activity sheet from the folder.

2. Read the cards and choose your favorite topic.

3. Make two lists—the three best things and the three worst things—about the topic on the activity sheet. Write the lists in complete sentences.

4. Check your work.

Writing Tips

A list is a series of items, names, numbers, ideas, etc., often written in a particular order. A list can be written as words, phrases, or sentences.

People write lists to remember things such as homework assignments or chores that need to get done. Students also write idea lists to prepare to write a paragraph, essay, or story.

Example

The 3 Best Things About Having a Pet

1. A pet like my dog Rusty keeps me company.
2. My pet and I go for long walks in the park.
3. My dog loves to retrieve Frisbees and balls for me.

The 3 Worst Things About Having a Pet

1. I have to remember to feed my dog twice a day.
2. My dog digs holes in our backyard, which makes my dad pretty mad.
3. I feel bad when I go to school and my dog has to stay home.

3 Best Things **3** Worst Things

About Staying
Up Late

3 Best Things **3** Worst Things

About a
Rainy Day

3 Best Things **3** Worst Things

About Being
a Girl

3 Best Things **3** Worst Things

About Being
a Boy

The Best and the Worst

The Best and the Worst

The Best and the Worst

The Best and the Worst

3 Best Things **3** Worst Things

About Working on a Group Project

3 Best Things **3** Worst Things

About Summer Camp

3 Best Things **3** Worst Things

About Helping Around the House

3 Best Things **3** Worst Things

About Having a Pet

The Best and the Worst

The Best and the Worst

The Best and the Worst

The Best and the Worst

3 Best Things   **3** Worst Things

About Recess

3 Best Things   **3** Worst Things

About Being an Adult

3 Best Things   **3** Worst Things

About the Way I Look

3 Best Things   **3** Worst Things

About Lunch at School

The Best and the Worst

The Best and the Worst

The Best and the Worst

The Best and the Worst

Synonym Power

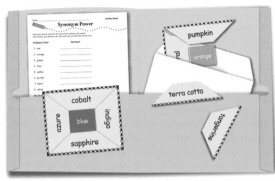

Puzzle Pieces

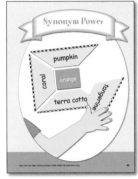

Folder Cover

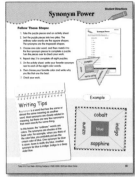

Student Directions

Preparing the Center

1. Prepare a folder following the directions on page 3.

   Cover—page 53

   Student Directions—page 55

   Puzzle Pieces—pages 57–63

2. Reproduce a supply of the activity sheet on page 52.

Using the Center

1. The student takes the puzzle pieces and an activity sheet from the folder.

2. Then the student sorts the puzzle pieces into two piles—squares (ordinary colors) and trapezoids (synonyms).

3. Next, the student chooses a color square. The student finds the four synonyms that match the color word to complete the puzzle. The puzzles are self-checking. How to recognize and use synonyms is modeled in the student directions.

4. The student repeats step 3 to complete all eight puzzles.

5. On the activity sheet, the student writes his or her favorite synonym for each of the eight color words.

6. Then the student picks one color and writes why it is his or her favorite.

7. Finally, the student evaluates the writing task using the checklist on the activity sheet.

Name _____

Activity Sheet

Synonym Power

Write your favorite synonym for each of the ordinary color words.
Then choose your favorite color and write why you like that one the best.

Ordinary Color	Synonym
1. red	_____
2. orange	_____
3. green	_____
4. blue	_____
5. yellow	_____
6. purple	_____
7. black	_____
8. white	_____

My favorite color is _____because_____

_____

_____

_____

_____

_____

✔ Check Your Work

◯ I chose my favorite synonyms for the eight color words.

◯ I chose my favorite color and wrote why I like it the best.

Synonym Power

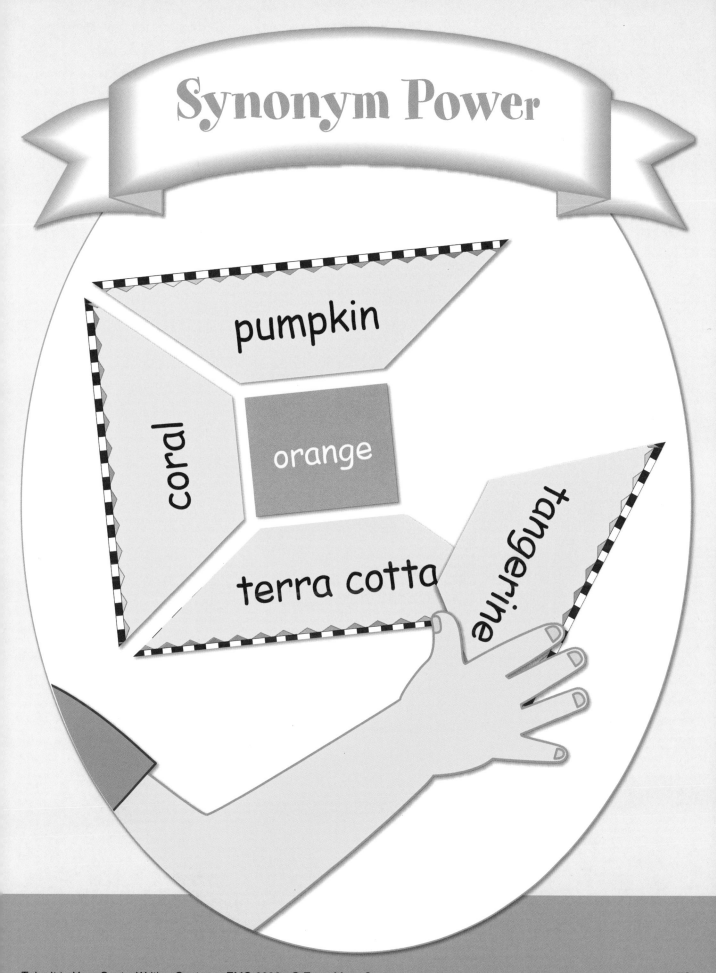

54

Synonym Power

Follow These Steps:

1. Take the puzzle pieces and an activity sheet.

2. Sort the puzzle pieces into two piles. The ordinary color words are the square shapes. The synonyms are the trapezoid shapes.

3. Choose one color word, and then match it to the four synonym pieces to complete a puzzle. Turn the pieces over to check your work.

4. Repeat step 3 to complete all eight puzzles.

5. On the activity sheet, write your favorite synonym next to each of the eight color words.

6. Then choose your favorite color and write why you like that one the best.

7. Check your work.

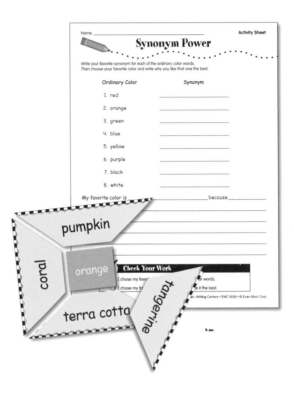

Writing Tips

A synonym is a word that has the same or almost the same meaning as another word. Most synonyms are closely related in meaning, but there are very few synonyms that mean *exactly* the same thing.

In this lesson, the "ordinary" words are colors. The synonyms are shades of the basic color. For example, when you think of the color blue, you probably picture the crayon color of blue. One synonym for *blue* is *azure*. Azure is really sky blue. Another synonym for *blue* is *indigo*. Indigo is a deep violet blue.

Example

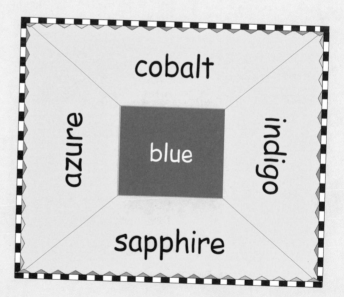

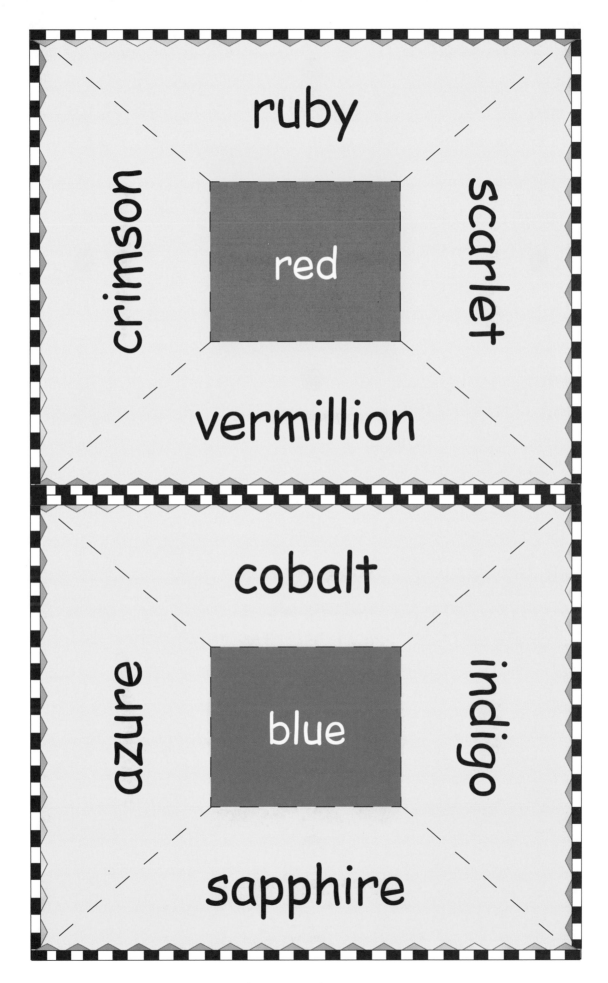

ruby

crimson

red

scarlet

vermillion

cobalt

azure

blue

indigo

sapphire

Synonym Power

Synonym Power

Synonym Power

Synonym Power

Synonym Power

Synonym Power

Synonym Power

Synonym Power

Synonym Power

Synonym Power

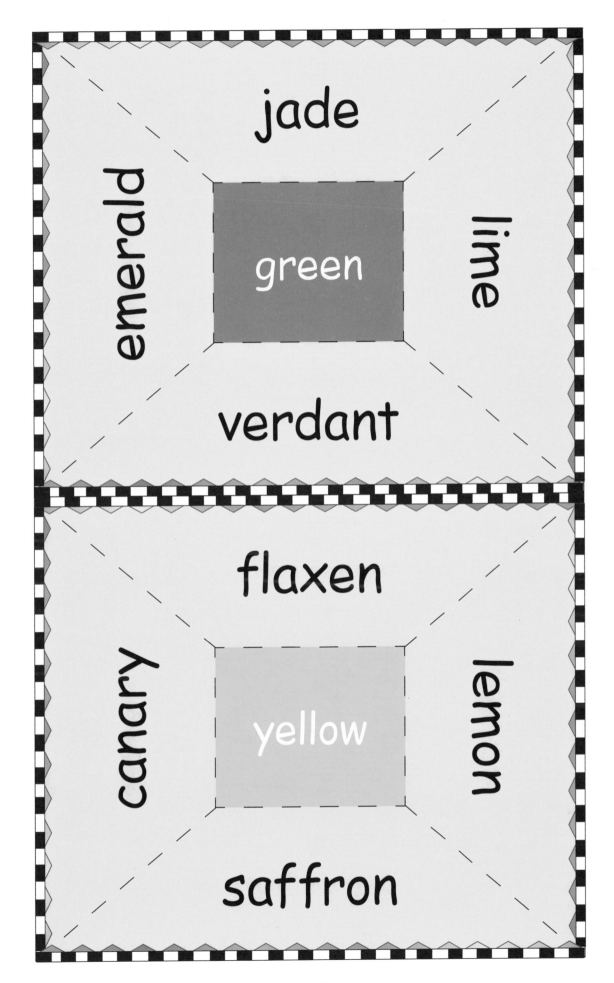

jade

emerald

green

lime

verdant

flaxen

canary

yellow

lemon

saffron

Synonym Power

Synonym Power

Synonym Power

Synonym Power

Synonym Power

Synonym Power

Synonym Power

Synonym Power

Synonym Power

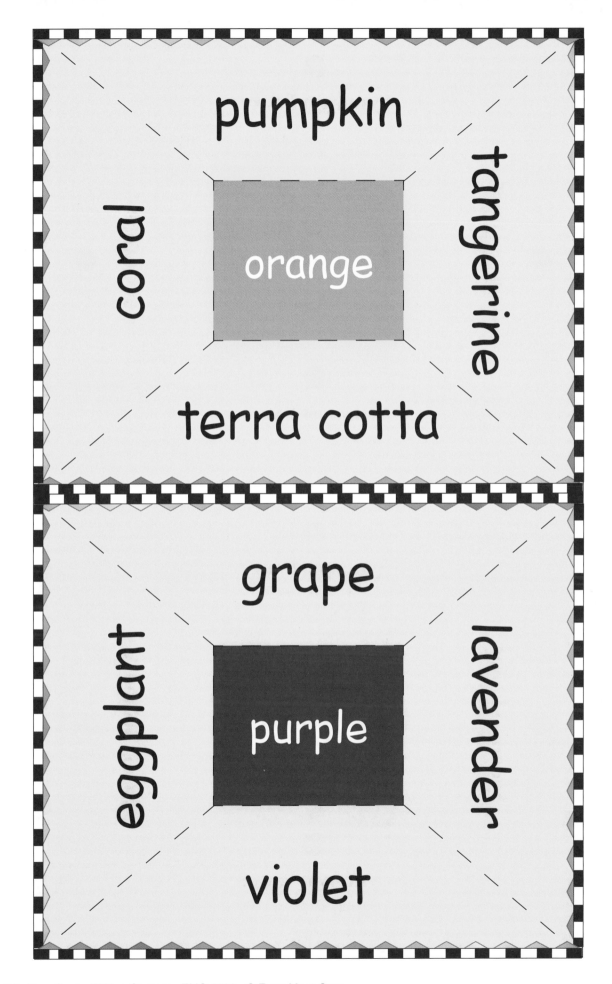

pumpkin

tangerine

coral

orange

terra cotta

grape

lavender

eggplant

purple

violet

Synonym Power

© Evan-Moor Corp. • EMC 6006

Synonym Power

© Evan-Moor Corp. • EMC 6006

Synonym Power

© Evan-Moor Corp. • EMC 6006

© Evan-Moor Corp. • EMC 6006

Synonym Power

Synonym Power

Synonym Power

© Evan-Moor Corp. • EMC 6006

Synonym Power

© Evan-Moor Corp. • EMC 6006

Synonym Power

© Evan-Moor Corp. • EMC 6006

Synonym Power

Synonym Power

© Evan-Moor Corp. • EMC 6006

© Evan-Moor Corp. • EMC 6006

Synonym Power

© Evan-Moor Corp. • EMC 6006

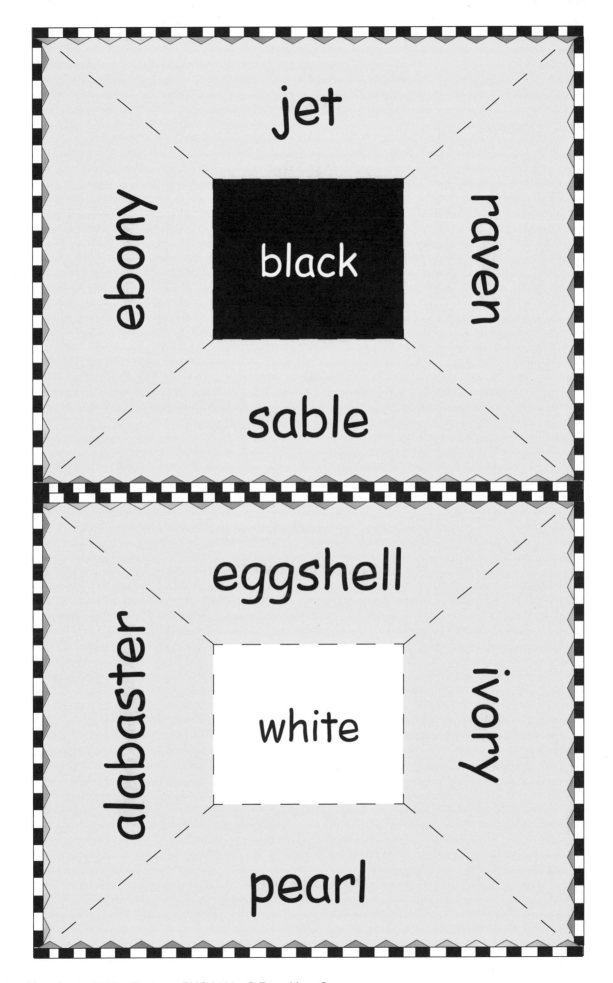

jet

ebony

black

raven

sable

eggshell

alabaster

white

ivory

pearl

Synonym Power

Synonym Power

Synonym Power

Synonym Power

Synonym Power

Synonym Power

Synonym Power

Synonym Power

Synonym Power

Synonym Power

Poetry Works

Task Cards

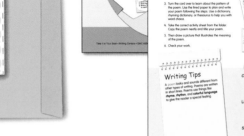

Folder Cover

Student Directions

Preparing the Center

1. Prepare a folder following the directions on page 3.

    Cover—page 69

    Student Directions—page 71

    Task Cards—pages 73–77

2. Reproduce a supply of the activity sheets on pages 66–68. Place a supply of lined paper in the folder, as well.

Using the Center

1. The student reads the poems on the cards and selects one pattern.

2. Next, the student uses the lined paper to plan an original poem following the pattern. How to write a specific kind of poem is modeled on the back of each card.

3. Then the student copies the poem onto the correct activity sheet. The student also draws a picture to illustrate the poem.

4. Finally, the student evaluates the writing task using the checklist on the activity sheet.

Poetry Works
Cinquain

Write a cinquain. Title the poem. Then draw a picture to illustrate the meaning of the poem.

_____
title

_____

_____

_____

_____

✓ Check Your Work

○ I followed the pattern to write a cinquain.

○ I titled my cinquain.

○ I illustrated my cinquain.

Poetry Works
Limerick

Write a limerick. Title the poem. Then draw a picture to illustrate the meaning of the poem.

_____
title

_____

_____

_____

_____

_____

✔ Check Your Work

○ I followed the pattern to write a limerick.

○ I titled my limerick.

○ I illustrated my limerick.

Poetry Works
Silly Triplet

Write a silly triplet. Title the poem. Then draw a picture to illustrate the meaning of the poem.

_____
title

_____

_____

_____

✓ Check Your Work

◯ I followed the steps to write a triplet.

◯ I titled my triplet.

◯ I illustrated my triplet.

Poetry Works

There once was a
man from Peru
Who found...

...t shout

...g it, too."

...le antelope
...lope
...g on a cantaloupe

Dragon
Scaly creature
Angrily breathing fire
Ferocious terror
of folklore
Serpent

Cinquain

A *cinquain* is a five-line poem. Each line has a specific number of syllables.

Line 1—one word

Line 2—two...

Silly Triplet

A *triplet* is a three-line rhyming poem.

1. Think ... character and describe it ... y way.

2. Make ... words and ph...

3. Use yo... e pl... yme ... the character.

... t rhyme.

Limerick

A *limerick* is an amusing verse of five lines. Line ... lines 3 and 4 rhyme. Line 5 refers to line 1. Line ... shorter than the other lines.

Line 1 _____

Line 2 _____

    Line 3 _____

    Line 4 _____

Line 5_____

1. Choose the name of a person, place, or th...
2. Write the first line following either patt...
    There was a _____
    There once was a _____
3. Write a second line that rhymes with...
4. Write two short lines that rhym...
5. Write a final line that rhym... to repeat part of yo...

Poetry Works

Follow These Steps:

1. Take the poetry cards and a sheet of lined paper.

2. Read the poems. Choose your favorite.

3. Turn the card over to learn about the pattern of the poem. Use the lined paper to plan and write your poem following the steps. Use a dictionary, rhyming dictionary, or thesaurus to help you with word choice.

4. Take the correct activity sheet from the folder. Copy the poem neatly and title your poem.

5. Then draw a picture that illustrates the meaning of the poem.

6. Check your work.

The green and purple antelope
Wore a gigantic envelope
While sitting on a cantaloupe

Writing Tips

A poem looks and sounds different from other types of writing. Poems are written in short lines. Poems use things like **rhyme**, **rhythm**, and **colorful language** to give the reader a special feeling.

Example

Cinquain
Turtle
Bashful critter
Slowly peeking, poking
Always cautious, never hasty
Tortoise

Limerick
There was a funny circus clown
Who liked to wear a wedding gown.
    It was quite a sight
    To see her in white
As she pranced around upside down.

Silly Triplet
The polka-dotted dinosaur
Chomping down on rich and poor
That's why he's called a carnivore

Dragon

Scaly creature

Angrily breathing fire

Ferocious terror
of folklore

Serpent

Brother

Older, bigger

Helping, sharing,
showing

Protecting his
little sister

Buddy

Cinquain

A *cinquain* is a five-line poem. Each line has a specific number of syllables.

Line 1—one word, two syllables, title

Line 2—two words, four syllables, describing the title

Line 3—three words, six syllables, expressing action

Line 4—four words, eight syllables, expressing a feeling

Line 5—one word, two syllables, a synonym for the title

Cinquain

A *cinquain* is a five-line poem. Each line has a specific number of syllables.

Line 1—one word, two syllables, title

Line 2—two words, four syllables, describing the title

Line 3—three words, six syllables, expressing action

Line 4—four words, eight syllables, expressing a feeling

Line 5—one word, two syllables, a synonym for the title

There once was a
man from Peru

Who found a dead
rat in his stew.

Said the waiter, "Don't shout

Or wave it about,

Or the rest will be wanting it, too."

There was a young farmer
from Leeds

Who swallowed six packets
of seeds.

It soon came to pass

He was covered with
grass,

And he couldn't sit down
for the weeds.

Limerick

A *limerick* is an amusing verse of five lines. Lines 1, 2, and 5 rhyme and lines 3 and 4 rhyme. Line 5 refers to line 1. Lines 3 and 4 are usually shorter than the other lines.

Line 1 _____

Line 2_____

      Line 3 _____

      Line 4 _____

Line 5_____

1. Choose the name of a person, place, or thing.
2. Write the first line following either pattern:

    There was a _____ named _____.

    There once was a _____ from _____.

3. Write a second line that rhymes with the first line.
4. Write two short lines that rhyme and tell something about your topic.
5. Write a final line that rhymes with the first two. You may want to repeat part of your first line.

Limerick

A *limerick* is an amusing verse of five lines. Lines 1, 2, and 5 rhyme and lines 3 and 4 rhyme. Line 5 refers to line 1. Lines 3 and 4 are usually shorter than the other lines.

Line 1 _____

Line 2_____

      Line 3 _____

      Line 4 _____

Line 5_____

1. Choose the name of a person, place, or thing.
2. Write the first line following either pattern:

    There was a _____ named _____.

    There once was a _____ from _____.

3. Write a second line that rhymes with the first line.
4. Write two short lines that rhyme and tell something about your topic.
5. Write a final line that rhymes with the first two. You may want to repeat part of your first line.

The green and purple antelope
Wore a gigantic envelope
While sitting on a cantaloupe

A dirty, messy troll
Was eating a jellyroll
While hanging from a pole

Silly Triplet

A *triplet* is a three-line rhyming poem.

1. Think of a character and describe it in a funny way.

2. Make a list of words and phrases that rhyme with the character.

3. Use your favorite phrases to write three lines that rhyme.

Silly Triplet

A *triplet* is a three-line rhyming poem.

1. Think of a character and describe it in a funny way.

2. Make a list of words and phrases that rhyme with the character.

3. Use your favorite phrases to write three lines that rhyme.

In the News

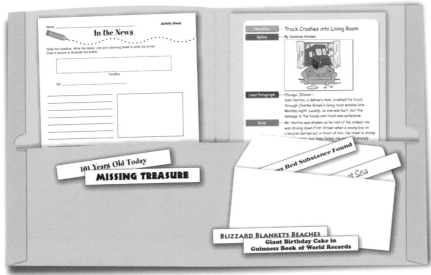

Task Strips

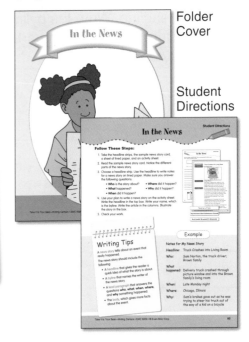

Folder Cover

Student Directions

Preparing the Center

1. Prepare a folder following the directions on page 3.

   Cover—page 81

   Student Directions—page 83

   Task Strips—pages 87 and 89

2. Laminate the sample news story card on page 85. Place the card in the right-hand pocket for student reference.

3. Reproduce a supply of the activity sheet on page 80. Provide a supply of lined paper for planning.

Using the Center

1. The student selects a headline strip, the sample news story card, a sheet of lined paper, and an activity sheet.

2. Then the student reads the sample news story to understand the parts of a news story.

3. Next, the student reads the headline strip and plans a news story on lined paper. How to write a newspaper article is modeled in the student directions.

4. On the activity sheet, the student copies the headline, writes the article, and illustrates the story.

5. Finally, the student evaluates the writing task using the checklist on the activity sheet.

Name _____

In the News

Write the headline. Write the byline. Use your planning sheet to write the article.
Draw a picture to illustrate the article.

headline

by _____

_____

_____

_____

_____

_____

_____

_____

_____

_____

✔ Check Your Work

○ I copied the headline.
○ I wrote my name as the byline.
○ I wrote a lead paragraph.
○ I wrote the body of the story.
○ I drew a picture to illustrate the story.

In the News

82

In the News

Follow These Steps:

1. Take the headline strips, the sample news story card, a sheet of lined paper, and an activity sheet.

2. Read the sample news story card. Notice the different parts of the news story.

3. Choose a headline strip. Use the headline to write notes for a news story on lined paper. Make sure you answer the following questions:

   - **Who** is the story about?
   - **What** happened?
   - **When** did it happen?
   - **Where** did it happen?
   - **Why** did it happen?

4. Use your plan to write a news story on the activity sheet. Write the headline in the top box. Write your name, which is the byline. Write the article in the columns. Illustrate the story in the box.

5. Check your work.

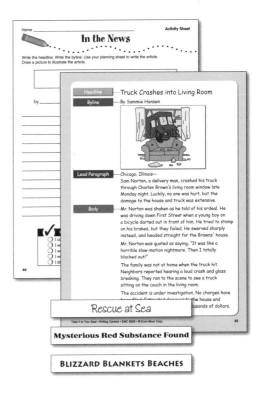

Writing Tips

A news story tells about an event that really happened.

The news story should include the following:

- A headline that gives the reader a quick idea of what the story is about.
- A byline that names the writer of the news story.
- A lead paragraph that answers the questions **who**, **what**, **when**, **where**, and **why** something happened.
- The body, which gives more facts about the event.

Example

Notes for My News Story

Headline: Truck Crashes into Living Room

Who: Sam Norton, the truck driver; Brown family

What happened: Delivery truck crashed through picture window and into the Brown family's living room

When: Late Monday night

Where: Chicago, Illinois

Why: Sam's brakes gave out as he was trying to steer his truck out of the way of a kid on a bicycle

84

Headline — # Truck Crashes into Living Room

Byline — By Sammie Hansen

Lead Paragraph — Chicago, Illinois—
Sam Norton, a delivery man, crashed his truck through Charles Brown's living room window late Monday night. Luckily, no one was hurt, but the damage to the house and truck was extensive.

Body — Mr. Norton was shaken as he told of his ordeal. He was driving down First Street when a young boy on a bicycle darted out in front of him. He tried to stomp on his brakes, but they failed. He swerved sharply instead, and headed straight for the Browns' house.

Mr. Norton was quoted as saying, "It was like a horrible slow-motion nightmare. Then I totally blacked out!"

The family was not at home when the truck hit. Neighbors reported hearing a loud crash and glass breaking. They ran to the scene to see a truck sitting on the couch in the living room.

The accident is under investigation. No charges have been filed. Estimated damages to the house and truck may run into hundreds of thousands of dollars.

Mysterious Red Substance Found

Rescue at Sea

BLIZZARD BLANKETS BEACHES

**Giant Birthday Cake in
Guinness Book of World Records**

101 Years Old Today

MISSING TREASURE

In the News

© Evan-Moor Corp. • EMC 6006

In the News

© Evan-Moor Corp. • EMC 6006

In the News

© Evan-Moor Corp. • EMC 6006

In the News

© Evan-Moor Corp. • EMC 6006

In the News

© Evan-Moor Corp. • EMC 6006

In the News

© Evan-Moor Corp. • EMC 6006

Truck Crashes into Living Room

Mountain Lion Spotted in Quiet Neighborhood

MAYOR'S OFFICE VANDALIZED BY SQUIRRELS

Underdogs Win Soccer Championship

Superman Spotted at Local Supermarket

Lion on the Loose

In the News

In the News

In the News

In the News

In the News

In the News

Fun Fables

Task Cards

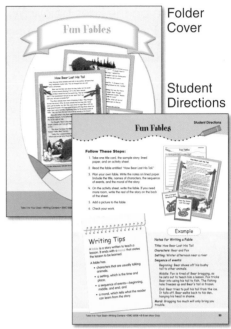

Folder Cover

Student Directions

Preparing the Center

1. Prepare a folder following the directions on page 3.

   Cover—page 93

   Student Directions—page 95

   Task Cards—pages 99–103

2. Reproduce a supply of the activity sheet on page 92. Also place lined paper in the folder.

3. Laminate the sample story on pages 97 and 98. Place the two-sided story card in the right-hand pocket of the folder for student reference.

Using the Center

1. The student takes the task cards, the sample story card, lined paper, and an activity sheet.

2. The student reads the sample fable to understand the parts of the genre.

3. Next, the student chooses a title card to write a fable. The student plans the story on lined paper. How to write a fable is modeled in the student directions.

4. Then the student writes and illustrates the fable on the activity sheet. The student also writes a moral, or lesson, for the story.

5. Finally, the student evaluates the writing task using the checklist on the activity sheet.

Name _____

Fun Fables

Write a fable on the lines below. Write the moral, or lesson, of the story.
Use the back of the page if you need more room. Illustrate the fable.

_____
title

_____

_____

_____

_____

_____

_____

_____

_____

Moral:

✓ Check Your Work

◯ I wrote a fable that had talking animals.
◯ I included a beginning, a middle, and an end.
◯ I wrote a moral that told what the reader can learn from the story.
◯ I illustrated my story.

Fun Fables

How Bear Lost His Tail

Long, long ago when animals could talk to one another, all bears had long, handsome, bushy tails. That all changed late one cold wintry afternoon.

Bear was terribly vain about his long, bushy tail. He would prance around showing it off to the other animals.

As Bear waved his tail, he would brag, "See my tail? Isn't it the handsomest tail you've ever seen? Don't you wish your tail was as wonderful?"

The other animals were tired of listening to Bear. They thought he was too proud. After all, many animals had nice long tails. Some were just as bushy, too. But they were afraid to anger Bear, with his huge powerful paws. His huge powerful paws with long sharp claws! An angry bear was a terrible, frightening thing. So the animals would all reply, "Yes, you have the best tail of all the animals in the forest."

One cold winter's day, Bear went out looking for something to fill his empty stomach. As he walked along the river, he saw Fox sitting on the ice by a pile of fish.

Fox thought, "Bear is too proud of that tail of his. He needs to be taught a lesson, and I am just the fox to do it. I think I'll play a trick on him."

The clever fox knew that Bear was hungry. Bear was hungry! "Hello, Bear," he said.

"Hello, Fox," answered Bear as he eyed Fox's pile of fish. "Where did you get all of those fish?"

"I caught them in the river," replied Fox.

...couldn't see any fishing pole. ...at did you use to catch

...ered Fox. "I dropped it into ...fish grabbed my tail, I pulled

...fishing that way. But there ...caught. Bear thought ...his stomach rumble. "Maybe ...fish for lunch."

...an Fox. After all, his tail ...und a spot on the ice.

...plained the wily fox.

Why a Dragon Breathes Fire

Why a Hummingbird Is So Small

Fun Fables

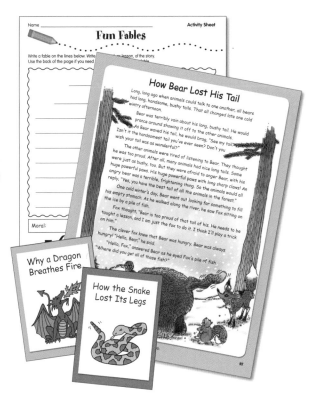

Follow These Steps:

1. Take one title card, the sample story, lined paper, and an activity sheet.

2. Read the fable entitled "How Bear Lost His Tail."

3. Plan your own fable. Write the notes on lined paper. Include the title, names of characters, the sequence of events, and the moral of the story.

4. On the activity sheet, write the fable. If you need more room, write the rest of the story on the back of the sheet.

5. Add a picture to the fable.

6. Check your work.

Writing Tips

A fable is a story written to teach a lesson. It ends with a moral that states the lesson to be learned.

A fable has:
- characters that are usually talking animals;
- a setting, which is the time and place;
- a sequence of events—beginning, middle, and end; and
- a moral, which tells what the reader can learn from the story.

Example

Notes for Writing a Fable

Title: How Bear Lost His Tail

Characters: Bear and Fox

Setting: Winter afternoon near a river

Sequence of events:

Beginning: Bear shows off his bushy tail to other animals.

Middle: Fox is tired of Bear bragging, so he sets out to teach him a lesson. Fox tricks Bear into using his tail to fish. The fishing hole freezes up and Bear's tail is frozen.

End: Bear tries to pull his tail from the ice. It falls off. Bear walks back to his den, hanging his head in shame.

Moral: Bragging too much will only bring you trouble.

How Bear Lost His Tail

Long, long ago when animals could talk to one another, all bears had long, handsome, bushy tails. That all changed late one cold wintry afternoon.

Bear was terribly vain about his long, bushy tail. He would prance around showing it off to the other animals.

As Bear waved his tail, he would brag, "See my tail? Isn't it the handsomest tail you've ever seen? Don't you wish your tail was as wonderful?"

The other animals were tired of listening to Bear. They thought he was too proud. After all, many animals had nice long tails. Some were just as bushy, too. But they were afraid to anger Bear, with his huge powerful paws. His huge powerful paws with long sharp claws! An angry bear was a terrible, frightening thing. So the animals would all reply, "Yes, you have the best tail of all the animals in the forest."

One cold winter's day, Bear went out looking for something to fill his empty stomach. As he walked along the river, he saw Fox sitting on the ice by a pile of fish.

Fox thought, "Bear is too proud of that tail of his. He needs to be taught a lesson, and I am just the fox to do it. I think I'll play a trick on him."

The clever fox knew that Bear was hungry. Bear was always hungry! "Hello, Bear," he said.

"Hello, Fox," answered Bear as he eyed Fox's pile of fish. "Where did you get all of those fish?"

"I caught them in the river," replied Fox.

Bear couldn't see any fishing pole. He asked, "What did you use to catch them?"

"I used my tail," answered Fox. "I dropped it into this hole in the ice. When a fish grabbed my tail, I pulled it out and the fish came, too."

Bear had never heard of fishing that way. But there was Fox with all of the fish he had caught. Bear thought about how good fish would taste. Just the thought made his stomach rumble. "Maybe I'll try this new way of fishing. I wouldn't mind some tasty fish for lunch."

Bear was sure that he would catch many more fish than Fox. After all, his tail was much longer and much bushier. Fox watched as Bear found a spot on the ice. Bear used his sharp claws to dig a hole through the ice.

"Now you must sit down with your back to the hole," explained the wily fox. "Then drop your handsome tail into the water. When you feel a fish bite, quickly pull out your tail. The fish will be caught. Remember, you must sit very still or you will scare the fish away." Then Fox picked up his own fish and walked away, laughing at the foolish bear.

Bear followed Fox's instructions. He sat down and dropped his tail into the water and waited for a fish to bite his tail. He sat still for so long that he fell asleep. While Bear slept, it grew much colder. Soon, the hole in the water froze shut.

When Bear woke up, he felt something holding his tail. Bear thought it was a fish at last. He jumped up and tried to pull his tail out of the water. As he tried to pull it out, the frozen tail snapped off. All that was left of his handsome, bushy tail was a small stump!

"My tail! My beautiful tail is gone!" he cried. The once proud bear had no tail and no fish. He sheepishly walked back to his den, hanging his head in shame.

And that is why to this day all bears have short tails.

> Moral: Bragging too much will only bring you trouble.

Take It to Your Seat—Writing Centers • EMC 6006 • © Evan-Moor Corp.

Why the Turtle Has a Hard Shell

Why a Dragon Breathes Fire

How a Lion Got Its Roar

How a Porcupine Got Its Quills

Fun Fables

© Evan-Moor Corp. • EMC 6006

Fun Fables

© Evan-Moor Corp. • EMC 6006

Fun Fables

© Evan-Moor Corp. • EMC 6006

Fun Fables

© Evan-Moor Corp. • EMC 6006

Why a Spider Has Eight Legs

Why a Hummingbird Is So Small

Why a Kangaroo Has a Pouch

How the Snake Lost Its Legs

Fun Fables

Fun Fables

Fun Fables

Fun Fables

Why a Mole Lives Underground

Why a Zebra Has Stripes

Why the Ostrich Forgot How to Fly

How the Canary Learned to Sing

Fun Fables

Fun Fables

Fun Fables

Fun Fables

Letter to the Editor

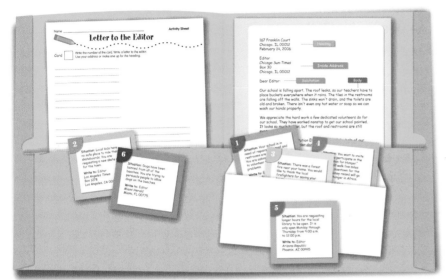

Task Cards

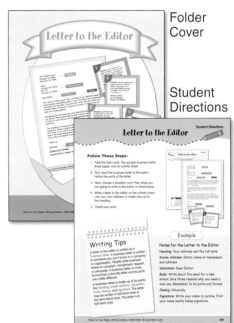

Folder Cover

Student Directions

Preparing the Center

1. Prepare a folder following the directions on page 3.

    Cover—page 107

    Student Directions—page 109

    Task Cards—pages 113 and 115

2. Reproduce a supply of the activity sheet on page 106. Also provide a supply of lined paper for planning.

3. Laminate the sample letter to the editor on page 111. Place the letter in the right-hand pocket for student reference.

Using the Center

1. The student takes the task cards, the sample letter, lined paper, and an activity sheet.

2. The student reads the sample letter to understand the parts of a business letter.

3. Next, the student chooses a situation card and plans what to say in a letter on lined paper.

4. Then the student uses the notes to write a letter to the editor on the activity sheet. How to write a business letter is modeled in the student directions.

5. Finally, the student evaluates the writing task using the checklist on the activity sheet.

Letter to the Editor

Card ☐ Write the number of the card. Write a letter to the editor.
Use your address or make one up for the heading.

_____

_____

_____

_____

_____

_____

_____ :

_____

_____

_____

_____

_____ ,

_____

_____

✓ Check Your Work

○ I wrote a business letter to the editor.
○ I included a heading and inside address.
○ I included a salutation and the body of the letter.
○ I included a closing, my signature, and my printed name.

Letter to the Editor

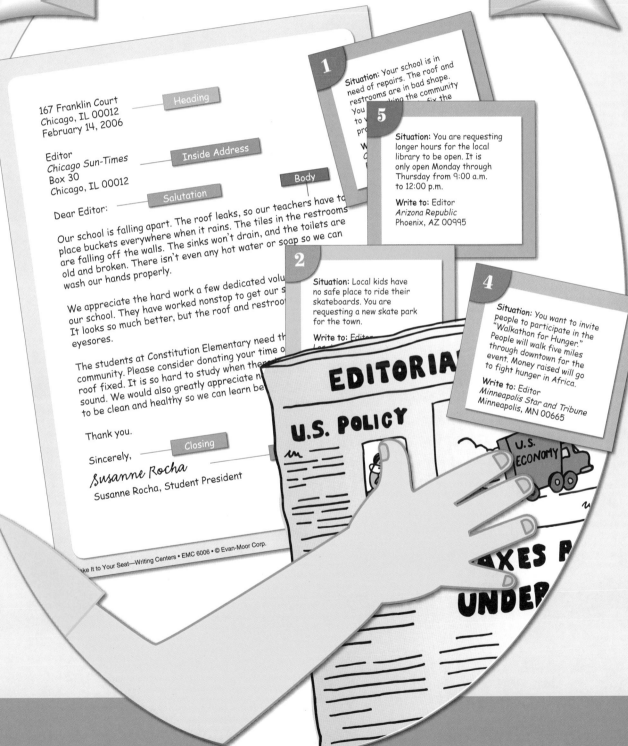

167 Franklin Court
Chicago, IL 00012
February 14, 2006

Heading

Editor
Chicago Sun-Times
Box 30
Chicago, IL 00012

Inside Address

Dear Editor:

Salutation

Body

Our school is falling apart. The roof leaks, so our teachers have to
place buckets everywhere when it rains. The tiles in the restrooms
are falling off the walls. The sinks won't drain, and the toilets are
old and broken. There isn't even any hot water or soap so we can
wash our hands properly.

We appreciate the hard work a few dedicated volu...
our school. They have worked nonstop to get our s...
It looks so much better, but the roof and restroo...
eyesores.

The students at Constitution Elementary need th...
community. Please consider donating your time o...
roof fixed. It is so hard to study when there...
sound. We would also greatly appreciate n...
to be clean and healthy so we can learn be...

Thank you.

Sincerely,

Closing

Susanne Rocha
Susanne Rocha, Student President

Take It to Your Seat—Writing Centers • EMC 6006 • © Evan-Moor Corp.

1 Situation: Your school is in need of repairs. The roof and restrooms are in bad shape. You ...king the community to ... fix the pro...

5 Situation: You are requesting longer hours for the local library to be open. It is only open Monday through Thursday from 9:00 a.m. to 12:00 p.m.

Write to: Editor
Arizona Republic
Phoenix, AZ 00995

2 Situation: Local kids have no safe place to ride their skateboards. You are requesting a new skate park for the town.

Write to: Editor
...

4 Situation: You want to invite people to participate in the "Walkathon for Hunger." People will walk five miles through downtown for the event. Money raised will go to fight hunger in Africa.

Write to: Editor
Minneapolis Star and Tribune
Minneapolis, MN 00665

Letter to the Editor

Follow These Steps:

1. Take the task cards, the sample business letter, lined paper, and an activity sheet.

2. First, read the business letter to the editor. Notice the parts of the letter.

3. Next, choose a situation card. Plan what you are going to write to the editor on lined paper.

4. Write a letter to the editor on the activity sheet. Use your own address or make one up for the heading.

5. Check your work.

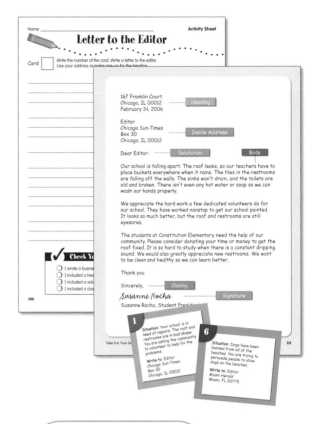

Writing Tips

A letter to the editor is written as a business letter. A business letter is written to someone you don't know in a company or organization. People write business letters to complain, compliment, request, or persuade. A business letter is more formal than a friendly letter and its parts are a little different.

A business letter is made up of six parts: the heading, inside address, salutation, body, closing, and signature. The letter may be written in full-block style or the semi-block style. This letter is in full-block style.

Example

Notes for the Letter to the Editor

Heading: Your address and the full date

Inside Address: Editor, name of newspaper, and address

Salutation: Dear Editor:

Body: Write about the need for a new school. Give three reasons why you need a new one. Remember to be polite and formal.

Closing: Sincerely,

Signature: Write your name in cursive. Print your name neatly below signature.

167 Franklin Court
Chicago, IL 00012   ————— Heading
February 14, 2006

Editor
Chicago Sun-Times   ————— Inside Address
Box 30
Chicago, IL 00012

Dear Editor: ————— Salutation   Body

Our school is falling apart. The roof leaks, so our teachers have to place buckets everywhere when it rains. The tiles in the restrooms are falling off the walls. The sinks won't drain, and the toilets are old and broken. There isn't even any hot water or soap so we can wash our hands properly.

We appreciate the hard work a few dedicated volunteers do for our school. They have worked nonstop to get our school painted. It looks so much better, but the roof and restrooms are still eyesores.

The students at Constitution Elementary need the help of our community. Please consider donating your time or money to get the roof fixed. It is so hard to study when there is a constant dripping sound. We would also greatly appreciate new restrooms. We want to be clean and healthy so we can learn better.

Thank you.

Sincerely,   ————— Closing

Susanne Rocha   ————— Signature
Susanne Rocha, Student President

1

Situation: Your school is in need of repairs. The roof and restrooms are in bad shape. You are asking the community to volunteer to help fix the problems.

Write to: Editor
Chicago Sun-Times
Box 30
Chicago, IL 00012

2

Situation: Local kids have no safe place to ride their skateboards. You are requesting a new skate park for the town.

Write to: Editor
Los Angeles Times
Box 1278
Los Angeles, CA 00117

3

Situation: There was a forest fire near your home. You would like to thank the local firefighters for saving your house.

Write to: Editor
Denver Post
Denver, CO 00233

4

Situation: You want to invite people to participate in the "Walkathon for Hunger." People will walk five miles through downtown for the event. Money raised will go to fight hunger in Africa.

Write to: Editor
Minneapolis Star and Tribune
Minneapolis, MN 00665

5

Situation: You are requesting longer hours for the local library to be open. It is only open Monday through Thursday from 9:00 a.m. to 12:00 p.m.

Write to: Editor
Arizona Republic
Phoenix, AZ 00995

6

Situation: Dogs have been banned from all of the beaches. You are trying to persuade people to allow dogs on the beaches.

Write to: Editor
Miami Herald
Miami, FL 00775

Letter to the Editor

Letter to the Editor

Letter to the Editor

Letter to the Editor

Letter to the Editor

Letter to the Editor

7

Situation: There is a vacant lot in your neighborhood. It is full of weeds and garbage. You would like to see the owners clean it up.

Write to: Editor
Washington Post
Washington, D.C. 00338

8

Situation: You would like to see a new stop sign placed at the corner of First Avenue and Irvine Street. The traffic goes too fast through the area. You saw a young child almost get hit.

Write to: Editor
Detroit Free Press
Detroit, MI 00099

9

Situation: You would like to recommend Dr. Jackie Carter as the "Citizen of the Year." She has donated her services at the Free Clinic. She treats children who can't afford to see a regular doctor. She is your hero.

Write to: Editor
St. Louis Post-Dispatch
St. Louis, MO 00765

10

Situation: You would like to invite the community to the school play called *Grease*. It will be held at Jackson Elementary on Friday and Saturday nights at 7:00 p.m. Tickets for adults are $6.00. Children under 12 are $3.00.

Write to: Editor
Boston Globe
Boston, MA 00655

11

Situation: You found dead fish washing up onto Waikiki Beach. You are concerned that humans are polluting the waters.

Write to: Editor
Honolulu Star-Bulletin
Honolulu, HI 00897

12

Situation: You would like to thank the anonymous person who returned your digital camera to the police station. Luckily, the camera had your name and telephone number on it. A police officer contacted you about the good deed.

Write to: Editor
Des Moines Register
Des Moines, IA 00162

Letter to the Editor

Letter to the Editor

Letter to the Editor

Letter to the Editor

Letter to the Editor

Letter to the Editor

Comic Strips

Task Cards

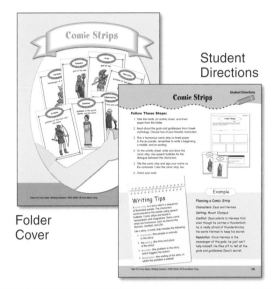

Student Directions

Folder Cover

Preparing the Center

1. Prepare a folder following the directions on page 3.

   Cover—page 119

   Student Directions—page 121

   Task Cards—pages 123–127

2. Reproduce a supply of the activity sheet on page 118. Also provide a supply of lined paper.

Using the Center

1. The student takes the cards and an activity sheet.

2. Then the student reads about the characters from Greek mythology on the cards.

3. Next, the student chooses two favorite characters.

4. The student uses the lined paper to plan a six-panel comic strip about the two characters. How to write a comic strip is modeled in the student directions.

5. On the activity sheet, the student then writes, draws, and colors a comic strip based on the two characters. The student also titles the comic strip.

6. Finally, the student evaluates the writing task using the checklist on the activity sheet.

Name _____

Comic Strips

Choose two characters from Greek mythology. Write, draw, and color a comic strip based on the two characters. Use speech bubbles for the dialogue. Title the comic strip and sign your name as the cartoonist.

_____   By _____
                title

Check Your Work

- ◯ I wrote a comic strip based on two characters from Greek mythology.
- ◯ I used humorous dialogue.
- ◯ I drew the scenes with the characters to reflect the dialogue.
- ◯ I titled the comic strip and signed my name.

Comic Strips

Comic Strips

Follow These Steps:

1. Take the cards, an activity sheet, and lined paper from the folder.

2. Read about the gods and goddesses from Greek mythology. Choose two of your favorite characters.

3. Plan a humorous comic strip on lined paper. In the six panels, remember to write a beginning, a middle, and an ending.

4. On the activity sheet, write and draw the comic strip. Use speech bubbles for the dialogue between the characters.

5. Title the comic strip and sign your name as the cartoonist. Color the comic strip, too.

6. Check your work.

Writing Tips

A comic strip is a story told in a sequence of illustrated panels. The characters communicate to the reader using speech bubbles. Comic strips are found in newspapers and magazines. Many comic strips are humorous, such as *Dennis the Menace*, *Garfield*, and *Zits*.

Like a story, a comic strip includes the following:

- characters (the people or animals in the story)
- the setting (the time and place of the story)
- a conflict (the problem in the story, which triggers the action)
- a resolution (the ending of the story, in which the problem is solved)

Example

Planning a Comic Strip

Characters: Zeus and Hermes

Setting: Mount Olympus

Conflict: Zeus admits to Hermes that even though he carries a thunderbolt, he is really afraid of thunderstorms. He wants Hermes to keep his secret.

Resolution: Since Hermes is the messenger of the gods, he just can't help himself. He flies off to tell all the gods and goddesses Zeus's secret.

Zeus

king of the gods

Athena

goddess of wisdom, law, and war

Hera

queen of the gods and the sky

Apollo

god of the sun, light,
music, archery, and healing

Athena was goddess of wisdom, law, and war. She was also the protector of cities. The city of Athens, Greece, was named after her. Her symbols were the owl and the olive tree.

Comic Strips

Zeus was the king of all the Greek gods. He lived on Mount Olympus. Zeus controlled the sky and weather and his family of gods. Zeus was fair, but if angered he threw thunderbolts at evildoers.

Comic Strips

Apollo was the god of the sun, light, truth, music, archery, and healing. His symbols were the lyre (a musical instrument) and the laurel tree.

Comic Strips

Hera was the wife of Zeus and queen of the sky. She was the goddess of all women and mothers and of marriage. Hera had three symbols: the cow, a pomegranate, and a peacock.

Comic Strips

Hermes

messenger of the gods

Poseidon

god of the sea

Ares

god of war

Aphrodite

goddess of love and beauty

Poseidon was the god of the sea and all water. He controlled storms, sea monsters, and earthquakes. Poseidon could protect or destroy ships. His symbols were a trident, dolphins, and horses.

Comic Strips

Hermes was the messenger of the gods. He reported events on Earth to the gods. Hermes wore a winged hat and winged shoes and carried a staff.

Comic Strips

Aphrodite was the goddess of love and beauty. She inspired love and protected people that were in love. Her symbols were doves, roses, sparrows, dolphins, and rams.

Comic Strips

Ares was the god of war. He was brave, angry, and terrible. Ares protected the soldiers on the fields. His symbols were a burning torch, a spear, dogs, and vultures.

Comic Strips

Artemis

goddess of the hunt and
the moon

Demeter

goddess of the earth,
plants, and harvests

Hephaestus

god of fire and armor

Hestia

goddess of the hearth
and the home

Demeter was the goddess of the earth, plants, and harvests. She protected the crops in the fields. Her daughter, Persephone, helped Demeter. Her symbol was a sheaf of wheat or barley.

Comic Strips

Artemis was the goddess of the hunt and the moon. She protected young girls and wild animals. Her symbols were the bow and arrow, deer, dogs, and the cypress tree.

Comic Strips

Hestia was the goddess of the hearth and home. She protected people's homes from evil. Every family had a shrine dedicated to her. She is often shown sitting in front of a wood fire.

Comic Strips

Hephaestus was the god of fire and armor. He protected craftsmen and metalsmiths while they worked on bronze weapons and tools. His symbols were a hammer and an anvil.

Comic Strips

Plan a Story

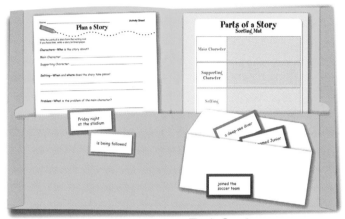

Task Cards

Folder Cover

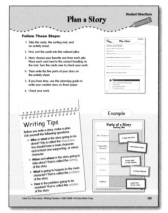

Student Directions

Preparing the Center

1. Prepare a folder following the directions on page 3.

    Cover—page 131

    Student Directions—page 133

    Sorting Mat—page 135

    Task Cards—pages 137–145

2. Reproduce a supply of the activity sheet on page 130. Also place a supply of lined paper in the folder.

Using the Center

1. The student takes the cards, the sorting mat, and an activity sheet from the folder.

2. Then the student looks through the cards and selects one of each color—main character, supporting character, setting, problem, and solution.

3. Next, the student reads each card and places it next to the correct heading on the mat. The cards are self-checking. The parts of a story are defined in the student directions.

4. Then the student writes the parts of the story on the activity sheet.

5. Finally, the student evaluates the writing task using the checklist on the activity sheet.

6. If there is time, the student uses this planning sheet to write a creative story on lined paper.

Name _____

Plan a Story

Write the parts of a story from the sorting mat.
If you have time, write a story on lined paper.

Characters—Who is the story about?

Main Character: _____

Supporting Character: _____

Setting—When and **where** does the story take place?

_____

_____

Problem—What is the problem of the main character?

_____

Solution—How does the problem get solved?

_____

✔ Check Your Work

○ I chose a main character and a supporting character.

○ I chose a setting.

○ I chose a problem and a solution.

○ I am ready to write my story.

Plan a Story

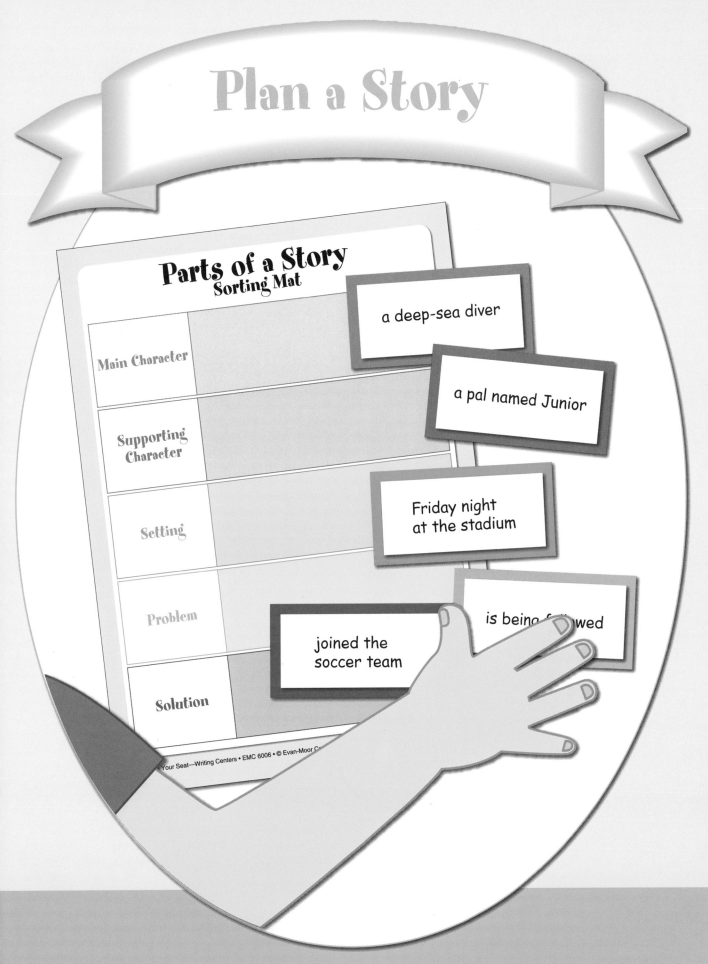

Parts of a Story
Sorting Mat

Main Character	
Supporting Character	
Setting	
Problem	
Solution	

a deep-sea diver

a pal named Junior

Friday night at the stadium

joined the soccer team

is being followed

Your Seat—Writing Centers • EMC 6006 • © Evan-Moor C

Plan a Story

Follow These Steps:

1. Take the cards, the sorting mat, and an activity sheet.

2. First, sort the cards into five colored piles.

3. Next, choose your favorite one from each pile. Place each card next to the correct heading on the mat. Turn the cards over to check your work.

4. Then write the five parts of your story on the activity sheet.

5. If you have time, use this planning guide to write your creative story on lined paper.

6. Check your work.

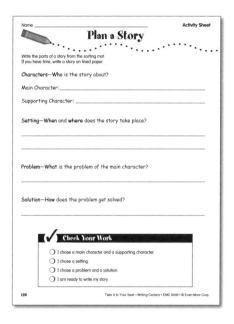

Name _____   Activity Sheet

Plan a Story

Write the parts of a story from the sorting mat.
If you have time, write a story on lined paper.

Characters—**Who** is the story about?

Main Character: _____

Supporting Character: _____

Setting—**When** and **where** does the story take place?

_____

_____

Problem—**What** is the problem of the main character?

_____

Solution—**How** does the problem get solved?

_____

✓ **Check Your Work**

○ I chose a main character and a supporting character.
○ I chose a setting.
○ I chose a problem and a solution.
○ I am ready to write my story.

130   Take It to Your Seat—Writing Centers • EMC 6006 • © Evan-Moor Corp.

Writing Tips

Before you write a story, make a plan. Ask yourself the following questions:

- **Who** or **what** is the story going to be about? This is called the characters. You should have a main character and at least one supporting, or minor, character.

- **When** and **where** is the story going to take place? That is called the setting of the story.

- **What** is going to happen to the main character? That is called the problem of the story.

- **How** is the problem going to be resolved? That is called the solution of the story.

Example

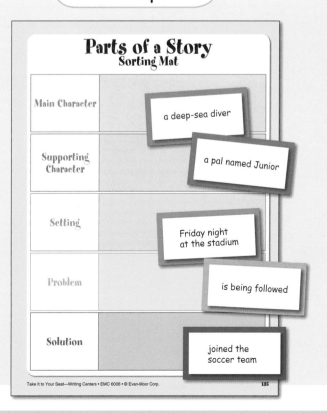

Parts of a Story
Sorting Mat

Main Character	a deep-sea diver
Supporting Character	a pal named Junior
Setting	Friday night at the stadium
Problem	is being followed
Solution	joined the soccer team

Take It to Your Seat—Writing Centers • EMC 6006 • © Evan-Moor Corp.   135

Parts of a Story
Sorting Mat

Main Character	
Supporting Character	
Setting	
Problem	
Solution	

136

an astronomer
named Mr. Know

a deep-sea diver

Johnnie the
new kid in town

the quarterback of
the football team

a nearsighted
paleontologist

a movie actress
named Phoebe LaFoy

a boy genius

a detective named
Snoopy Jones

Main Character

Plan a Story

© Evan-Moor Corp. • EMC 6006

Main Character

Plan a Story

© Evan-Moor Corp. • EMC 6006

Main Character

Plan a Story

© Evan-Moor Corp. • EMC 6006

Main Character

Plan a Story

© Evan-Moor Corp. • EMC 6006

Main Character

Plan a Story

© Evan-Moor Corp. • EMC 6006

Main Character

Plan a Story

© Evan-Moor Corp. • EMC 6006

Main Character

Plan a Story

© Evan-Moor Corp. • EMC 6006

Main Character

Plan a Story

© Evan-Moor Corp. • EMC 6006

an alien from Mars

a trained dolphin named Blue

a dog named Rusty

a pal named Junior

the local librarian

a makeup artist

a buggy little sister

a witness named Mrs. Winters

Supporting Character

Plan a Story

Supporting Character

Plan a Story

Supporting Character

Plan a Story

Supporting Character

Plan a Story

Supporting Character

Plan a Story

Supporting Character

Plan a Story

Supporting Character

Plan a Story

Supporting Character

Plan a Story

in the year 3000
far out in space

on a moonless night
in the Pacific Ocean

the first day at
Lincoln Elementary

Friday night
at the stadium

on a hot summer day
at the site called
Dinosaur Mounds

on opening night
at the theater

the final day of the
National Spelling Bee

midnight at the
abandoned house

Setting

Plan a Story

Setting

Plan a Story

Setting

Plan a Story

Setting

Plan a Story

Setting

Plan a Story

Setting

Plan a Story

Setting

Plan a Story

Setting

Plan a Story

Earth's moon
has disappeared
from sight

has had a
boating accident

has moved
into a run-down
apartment building

the home team
has just lost its
most valuable player

has fallen into
a deep hole

a tornado is
heading to town

has lost all
memory of what
happened yesterday

is being followed

Problem

Plan a Story

© Evan-Moor Corp. • EMC 6006

Problem

Plan a Story

© Evan-Moor Corp. • EMC 6006

Problem

Plan a Story

© Evan-Moor Corp. • EMC 6006

Problem

Plan a Story

© Evan-Moor Corp. • EMC 6006

Problem

Plan a Story

© Evan-Moor Corp. • EMC 6006

Problem

Plan a Story

© Evan-Moor Corp. • EMC 6006

Problem

Plan a Story

© Evan-Moor Corp. • EMC 6006

Problem

Plan a Story

© Evan-Moor Corp. • EMC 6006

flew off in
a spacecraft

was rescued by
the Coast Guard

joined the
soccer team

they had a
big pizza party

was found wandering
through the park

moved to the mansion
on the hill

got second prize
in the contest

has discovered the
secret passageway

Solution

Plan a Story

Solution

Plan a Story

Solution

Plan a Story

Solution

Plan a Story

Solution

Plan a Story

Solution

Plan a Story

Solution

Plan a Story

Solution

Plan a Story

A Personal Narrative

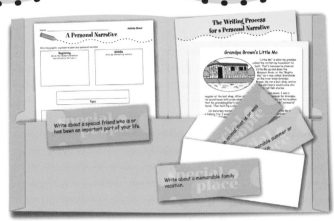

Task Cards

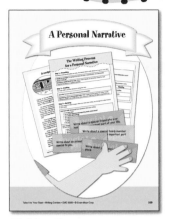

Folder Cover

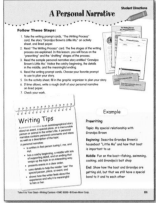

Student Directions

Preparing the Center

1. Prepare a folder following the directions on page 3.

   Cover—page 149

   Student Directions—page 151

   Task Cards—pages 157–161

2. Reproduce a supply of the activity sheet on page 148. Also provide a supply of lined paper.

3. Laminate "The Writing Process" card on pages 153 and 154 and the sample narrative entitled "Grandpa Brown's Little Mo" on page 155. Place the cards in the right-hand pocket for student reference.

Using the Center

1. The student reads "The Writing Process."

   Note: For this center, the student will focus on the prewriting and rough draft stages of the process. If desired, the teacher may choose to have the student follow the process through all five stages.

2. Next, the student reads the sample personal narrative.

3. Then the student reads the writing prompt cards and chooses his or her favorite.

4. On the activity sheet, the student plans his or her personal narrative using the graphic organizer. How to plan and write a personal narrative is modeled in the student directions and on "The Writing Process" card.

5. If time allows, the student uses the graphic organizer as a guide to write a rough draft of the story on lined paper.

6. Finally, the student evaluates the writing task using the checklist on the activity sheet.

Name _____

A Personal Narrative

Fill in the graphic organizer to plan your personal narrative.

Beginning
(Grab the reader's attention
and introduce the topic.)

Middle
(Provide interesting details.)

_____

Topic

End
(Remind the reader why the story is memorable and meaningful.)

✔ Check Your Work

- ◯ I chose a topic that was important to me.
- ◯ I wrote a catchy idea for the beginning of my story.
- ◯ I listed interesting details to include in my story.
- ◯ I wrote an idea for an ending that wraps up the story.
- ◯ I am ready to write my rough draft.

A Personal Narrative

The Writing Process for a Personal Narrative

Step 1—Prewriting

Prewriting is what you do before you write. You decide what to write about and organize your ideas.

Decide on your topic. Is it going to be about an event, a special place, or a memorable person in your life?

Brainstorm details that fit the topic. Make a list of details you remember about the topic. Organize the details on a graphic organizer.

Step 2—Drafting

The rough draft is your first attempt at writing the story.

Just write! Turn your ideas into sentences and paragraphs.

Organize the story in chronological order. Write a beginning that grabs the reader. Provide interesting details in the middle of the story. At the end, write why the topic is important to you.

Step 3—Revising

To revise means to make changes. When you revise your writing, you change it to make it clearer for your reader:

Read your draft. Ask yourself these questions about your writing:

- Is my topic clear?
- Are my topic sentences and supporting details stated clearly?
- Do I need to add anything?
- Do I nee[...]
- Do I ne[...] or easie[...]
- Do I ne[...]

Have someone[...]
Ask your frien[...]

- What is[...]
- Tell me[...]
- Tell me[...]

Grandpa[...]

regular at the bait shop. [...]
He would beam with pride [...]
that his granddaughter's [...]
Sandi. Then he'd flip a si[...]

On Saturday morning [...]
a fishing trip. I would g[...]
be an expert fisherman [...]
Those ugly little fish w[...]
masterfully on the bu[...]
fried potatoes filled o[...]
life!"

Then Grandpa wou[...]
go swimming. It was [...]
waters of the Missou[...]
until my arms ached.[...]
she would surprise [...]
with delight as he w[...]

After four year[...]
Grandpa was heart[...]
her up again, but G[...]
90 years [...]

So no[...]
The you[...]
Grandp[...]
over at[...]
special[...]

Write about a special friend who is or
has [...] important part of your life.

Write about a special family member
[...] important part

Write about an animal [...] special to you.

Write about y[...] special [...]
place.

A Personal Narrative

Follow These Steps:

1. Take the writing prompt cards, "The Writing Process" card, the story "Grandpa Brown's Little Mo," an activity sheet, and lined paper.

2. Read "The Writing Process" card. The five stages of the writing process are explained. In this lesson, you will focus on the "prewriting" and the "drafting" stages of the process.

3. Read the sample personal narrative story entitled "Grandpa Brown's Little Mo." Notice the catchy beginning, the details in the middle, and the meaningful ending.

4. Read the writing prompt cards. Choose your favorite prompt to use to plan your story.

5. On the activity sheet, fill in the graphic organizer to plan your story.

6. If time allows, write a rough draft of your personal narrative on lined paper.

7. Check your work.

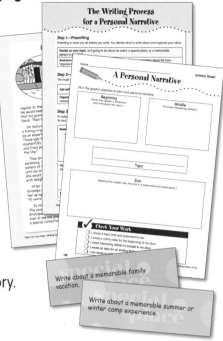

Writing Tips

A personal narrative is an autobiographical story about an event, a special place, or a memorable person or animal in the writer's life. A personal narrative contains personal comments and ideas as well as a description of the topic.

A personal narrative:

- is written in first person (using *I*, *me*, and *my*);
- has a catchy beginning, a middle with lots of supporting detail, and an ending that wraps up the topic in an interesting way;
- presents events in a clear order;
- uses details to help the reader "see" the special person, place, or event; and
- shows how the writer feels about the experience and why it is meaningful to him or her.

Example

Prewriting

Topic: My special relationship with Grandpa Brown

Beginning: Describe Grandpa Brown's houseboat "Little Mo" and how that boat is important to us

Middle: Fun on the boat—fishing, swimming, cooking; add Grandpa's bait shop

End: Show how the boat and Grandpa are getting old, but that we still have a special bond to it and to each other

The Writing Process for a Personal Narrative

Step 1—Prewriting

Prewriting is what you do before you write. You decide what to write about and organize your ideas.

> **Decide on your topic.** Is it going to be about an event, a special place, or a memorable person in your life?

> **Brainstorm details that fit the topic.** Make a list of details you remember about the topic. Organize the details on a graphic organizer.

Step 2—Drafting

The rough draft is your first attempt at writing the story.

> **Just write!** Turn your ideas into sentences and paragraphs.

> **Organize the story in chronological order.** Write a beginning that grabs the reader. Provide interesting details in the middle of the story. At the end, write why the topic is important to you.

Step 3—Revising

To revise means to make changes. When you revise your writing, you change it to make it clearer for your reader.

> **Read your draft.** Ask yourself these questions about your writing:
>
> - Is my topic clear?
> - Are my topic sentences and supporting details stated clearly?
> - Do I need to add anything?
> - Do I need to cut any parts?
> - Do I need to change my language to make the piece more interesting or easier to understand?
> - Do I need to put things in a different order?

> **Have someone else read your draft.** A peer can help you make your writing better. Ask your friend to answer the following:
>
> - What is the main idea of my story?
> - Tell me which part you liked best. Why?
> - Tell me which part or parts of the story confused you.
> - Tell me how I can make it better.

> **Revise your story.**

Step 4—Editing

This is the point at which you check your story for errors.

Look for errors. Ask yourself these questions:
- Does each sentence begin with a capital letter?
- Does each sentence end with a period, a question mark, or an exclamation point?
- Did I use correct grammar?
- Did I check for spelling errors?
- Did I indent each new paragraph?

Use proofreading marks to show what you need to fix. Here are a few common marks:

Mark	Meaning
☰	Capitalize.
⊙	Add a period.
∧	Add a comma.

Mark	Meaning
~~sed~~	Fix the spelling.
∧	Add a word.
ℓ	Delete.

Step 5—Publishing

The last step is to write a final copy of your story.

Write your story correctly and neatly using a black or blue pen.

Share your story with an audience. Read it aloud to a family member or a friend.
Give a special person a copy of your personal narrative.

Grandpa Brown's Little Mo

"Little Mo" is what my grandpa called the rattletrap houseboat he built. That's because he steered Little Mo up and down the Missouri River, or the "Mighty Mo," as it was called. Everybody on the river knew Grandpa Brown. He ran a bait shop, and so all the old-timers would come into his shop to tell fish stories.

From the time I was seven, I was a regular at the bait shop. After school, I would catch crawdads for Grandpa. He would beam with pride when my bucket was full. He would tell his buddies that his granddaughter's nickname should really be "Crawdaddy" instead of Sandi. Then he'd flip a silver dollar at me for a job well done.

On Saturday mornings, Grandpa and Grandma would take Little Mo out on a fishing trip. I would go along for the ride. You would think Grandpa would be an expert fisherman, but actually he tended to catch only bullheads. Those ugly little fish were not that tasty, but Grandma would fry them up masterfully on the burner as we slowly moved along on the current. Fish and fried potatoes filled our stomachs. Grandpa would always say, "This is the life!"

Then Grandpa would anchor the boat on a sandbar just so I could go swimming. It was our little secret that he let me swim in the treacherous waters of the Missouri. The water was always murky, but I swam in circles until my arms ached. Grandma kept a watchful eye on me. Once in a while, she would surprise me and dive into the muddy waters. Grandpa chuckled with delight as he watched us come up with mud and gunk in our hair.

After four years of memories on the river, Little Mo finally fell apart. Grandpa was heartsick to lose the old girl. Grandpa was determined to fix her up again, but Grandma put a stop to that. After all, Grandpa was now 90 years old. Grandma worried about him and his bad hip.

So now what's left of Little Mo sits in the backyard of Grandpa's house. The younger grandkids pretend they are floating down the Missouri. Grandpa watches them with a melancholy look in his eyes. Then he glances over at me and gives me a wink. We know the two of us will always share a special connection with Little Mo.

Write about a special friend who is or has been an important part of your life.

Write about a special family member who is or has been an important part of your life.

Write about a special person you know or have met that is your hero.

Write about an animal that is or was special to you.

A Personal Narrative

A Personal Narrative

A Personal Narrative

A Personal Narrative

Write about a memorable family vacation.

Write about your special secret hiding place.

Write about a memorable summer or winter camp experience.

Write about what is special about your home.

A Personal Narrative

© Evan-Moor Corp. • EMC 6006

A Personal Narrative

© Evan-Moor Corp. • EMC 6006

A Personal Narrative

© Evan-Moor Corp. • EMC 6006

A Personal Narrative

© Evan-Moor Corp. • EMC 6006

Write about a memorable birthday celebration.

Write about a memorable wedding you attended.

Write about a memorable award ceremony you were part of.

Write about a memorable day at school.

A Personal Narrative

© Evan-Moor Corp. • EMC 6006

A Personal Narrative

© Evan-Moor Corp. • EMC 6006

A Personal Narrative

© Evan-Moor Corp. • EMC 6006

A Personal Narrative

© Evan-Moor Corp. • EMC 6006

Tongue Twisters

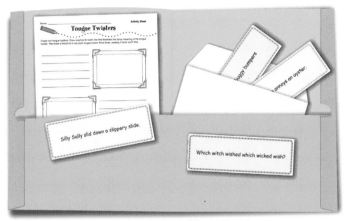

Task Cards

Folder Cover

Student Directions

Preparing the Center

1. Prepare a folder following the directions on page 3.

   Cover—page 165

   Student Directions—page 167

   Task Cards—pages 169–175

2. Reproduce a supply of the activity sheet on page 164.

Using the Center

1. The student takes the task cards and an activity sheet.

2. The student reads the tongue twisters on the cards. Encourage the student to read each one aloud.

3. Next, the student chooses a favorite to practice saying over and over again, saying it faster and faster each time.

4. Then the student writes two original tongue twisters. How to write a tongue twister is modeled in the student directions.

5. The student should also illustrate the two tongue twisters.

6. If time allows, the student asks a friend to say each tongue twister three times, getting faster each time.

7. Finally, the student evaluates the writing task using the checklist on the activity sheet.

Name _____

Tongue Twisters

Create two tongue twisters. Draw a picture for each one that illustrates the funny meaning of the tongue twister. Then have a friend try to say each tongue twister three times, reading it faster each time.

_____

_____

_____

_____

_____

_____

_____

_____

✔ Check Your Work

◯ I wrote two tongue twisters.

◯ I illustrated the two tongue twisters.

◯ A friend said the tongue twisters really fast.

Tongue Twisters

Rubber baby buggy bu

Which witch wished which wicked wish?

A noisy noise annoys an

Silly Sally slid down a slippery slide.

Tongue Twisters

Follow These Steps:

1. Take the cards and an activity sheet.

2. Read the tongue twisters. Enjoy reading them aloud.

3. Choose your favorite tongue twister. Say it really fast three times in a row.

4. On the activity sheet, write two of your own tongue twisters. Illustrate them, too.

5. Have a friend say each tongue twister three times, saying it faster each time.

6. Check your work.

Writing Tips

A tongue twister is a silly phrase, sentence, or group of sentences that is hard to say fast. That is because a tongue twister contains a tricky combination of words. Some use alliteration. Alliteration is the repetition of consonant sounds. Other tongue twisters use words that have similar sounds.

Read the two familiar tongue twisters at right.

Example

Alliteration

Peter Piper picked a peck of pickled peppers.

Similar Sounds

She sells seashells down by the seashore.

Rubber baby buggy bumpers

A noisy noise annoys an oyster.

Betty and Bob brought back blue balloons from the big bazaar.

Friendly Frank flips fine flapjacks.

Tongue Twisters

© Evan-Moor Corp. • EMC 6006

Tongue Twisters

© Evan-Moor Corp. • EMC 6006

Tongue Twisters

© Evan-Moor Corp. • EMC 6006

Tongue Twisters

© Evan-Moor Corp. • EMC 6006

Silly Sally slid down a slippery slide.

Which witch wished which wicked wish?

Lesser leather never weathered
wetter weather better.

I scream, you scream,
we all scream for ice cream.

Tongue Twisters

Tongue Twisters

Tongue Twisters

Tongue Twisters

Six shimmering sharks
sharply striking shins

Seven silly swans swam
silently seaward.

Great gray geese graze in
the green, green grass.

I thought a thought. But the thought
I thought wasn't the thought
I thought I thought.

Tongue Twisters

Tongue Twisters

Tongue Twisters

Tongue Twisters

A big black bug bit a big black bear,
and made the big black bear bleed blood.

While we were walking, we were
watching window washers wash
Washington's windows with warm
washing water.

Pick a partner and practice passing,
for if you pass proficiently, perhaps
you'll play professionally.

Betty Botter had some butter.
"But," she said, "this butter's bitter.
If I bake this bitter butter, it would
make my batter bitter."

Tongue Twisters

Tongue Twisters

Tongue Twisters

Tongue Twisters

Editing Workshop

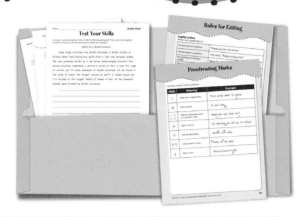

Folder Cover

Student Directions

Preparing the Center

1. Prepare a folder following the directions on page 3.

    Cover—page 181

    Student Directions—page 183

    Answer Key—pages 189–192

2. Reproduce a supply of the activity sheets on pages 178–180.

3. Laminate the "Proofreading Marks" chart on page 185 for student reference. Place it in the pocket for students to use with the practice pages.

4. Laminate the "Rules for Editing" charts on pages 187 and 188. Place the two-sided chart in the pocket for students to use as reference.

5. Provide red pens for editing tasks.

Using the Center

1. The student selects one page of editing tasks to practice. *Note: The teacher may wish to choose which language skills the student needs to practice.*

2. First, the student uses the "Proofreading Marks" chart as a guide for making the corrections on the practice page. The student also may refer to the "Rules for Editing" chart as a guide. How to edit is modeled in the student directions.

3. Next, the student uses the answer key to check his or her answers for that practice page.

4. Then the student completes the activity sheet on page 178. The student uses the answer key to check his or her answers for the activity sheet.

5. Finally, the student evaluates the editing task using the checklist on the activity sheet.

Test Your Skills

In red pen, use proofreading marks to edit the following paragraph. Then write the paragraph correctly on the lines. Use the answer key to check your answers.

What Is a Shield Volcano?

many large volcanoes are shield volcanoes a shield volcano is formed when free-flowing lava spills from a vent and spreads widely the lava gradually builds up a low broad dome-shaped mountain the domed mountain resembles a warrior's shield so that is how this type of volcano got its name examples of shield volcanoes can be found in the state of hawaii the largest volcano on earth is called mauna loa it is located on the largest island of hawaii in fact all the hawaiian islands were formed by shield volcanoes

_____

_____

_____

_____

_____

_____

_____

✓ Check Your Work

◯ I used proofreading marks to correct the paragraph.
◯ I copied the paragraph correctly.
◯ I used the answer key to check my answers.

Name _____

Edit Practice 1

Capitals and Punctuation for Dialogue

1. when are we going to new york to see the statue of liberty susanne asked her parents

2. i think we should have pizza cookies and lemonade for our party zachary said to the others on the committee

3. carolina exclaimed excitedly i was elected class president

4. feed the dog right now tom demanded

5. mrs franklin announced to the class our field trip is tomorrow so please be at the school at 800

Edit Practice 2

162 first avenue

bismarck nd 00066

august 8 2007

mr mario guzman

principal

lincoln elementary

box 444

bismarck nd 00066

dear mr guzman

    my name is mrs samantha jones my son kevin will be a new sixth-grade student at your school kevin has been playing the trumpet for two years he would like to play in the school band i understand that band lessons are given the last period of the day i hope you can arrange his schedule so that he can participate in the band

thank you

sincerely

mrs samantha jones

Editing Workshop

Editing Workshop

Follow These Steps:

1. Choose one of the "Edit Practice" pages.

2. Next, use a red pen to make the correct proofreading marks on the edit practice page.

   - Use the "Proofreading Marks" chart to help you.

   - Use the two-sided "Rules for Editing" chart to help you.

3. Check your work on the edit practice page using the answer key.

4. Then complete the "Test Your Skills" activity sheet.

5. Finally, check your work on the activity sheet using the answer key.

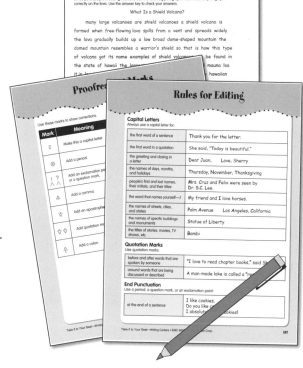

Writing Tips

It is important to edit a piece of writing before making a final copy. To edit is to check for mistakes.

Editors use special proofreading marks to show the mistakes that need to be fixed. Editors follow the rules of capitalization and punctuation to guide them in that process.

Look at the example.

Example

Not Edited
may i go with you to disneyland
asked jonathon

Edited
"may i go with you to disneyland?"
asked jonathon.

Final Copy
"May I go with you to Disneyland?"
asked Jonathon.

Proofreading Marks

Use these marks to show corrections.

Mark	Meaning	Example
≡	Make this a capital letter.	First prize went to maria.
⊙	Add a period.	It was late⊙
! ?	Add an exclamation point or a question mark.	Help! Can you help me?
∧	Add a comma.	On Monday, we will go to school.
∨	Add an apostrophe.	That's Lil's bike.
⌄⌄ ⌄⌄	Add quotation marks.	"Come in," he said.
∧	Add a colon.	Alex arrived at 4:00.

Rules for Editing

Capital Letters
Always use a capital letter for:

the first word of a sentence	Thank you for the letter.
the first word in a quotation	She said, "Today is beautiful."
the greeting and closing in a letter	Dear Juan, Love, Sherry
the names of days, months, and holidays	Thursday, November, Thanksgiving
people's first and last names, their initials, and their titles	Mrs. Cruz and Felix were seen by Dr. S.C. Lee.
the word that names yourself—*I*	My friend and I love horses.
the names of streets, cities, and states	Palm Avenue Los Angeles, California
the names of specific buildings and monuments	Statue of Liberty
the titles of stories, movies, TV shows, etc.	Bambi

Quotation Marks
Use quotation marks:

before and after words that are spoken by someone	"I love to read chapter books," said Sharon.
around words that are being discussed or described	A man-made lake is called a "reservoir."

End Punctuation
Use a period, a question mark, or an exclamation point:

at the end of a sentence	I like cookies. Do you like cookies? I absolutely love cookies!

Commas

Always use a comma to separate:

a city and a state	Miami, Florida
the date from the year	December 25, 2006
the greeting and closing of a letter	Dear Jane, Yours truly,
two adjectives that tell about the same noun	Nico is a clever, smart boy.

Use a comma to show a pause:

between three or more items in a series	Juan likes pizza, spaghetti, and lasagna.
between the words spoken by someone and the rest of the sentence	"I know," answered Maya.
after a short introductory phrase	After all that candy, nobody was hungry for cake.

Apostrophes

Add an apostrophe:

when there is one owner, add an apostrophe first, and then add an s	cat + 's = cat's The cat's dish is empty.
when there is more than one owner, add an s first and then an apostrophe	cats + ' = cats' All the cats' dishes were empty.
when you put two words together to make a contraction	he + is = he's Now he's on the table.

Colons

Add a colon:

after the salutation of a business letter	Dear Ms. Matthews:
between numerals indicating time	Meet me at the park at 12:00.
to introduce a list	Please bring the following: paper plates, plastic cups, and silverware.

Take It to Your Seat—Writing Centers • EMC 6006 • © Evan-Moor Corp.

Editing Workshop
Answer Key

Editing Workshop
Answer Key

Edit Practice 1

Capitals and Punctuation for Dialogue

1. "when are we going to new york to see the statue of liberty?" susanne asked her parents.

2. "i think we should have pizza, cookies, and lemonade for our party," zachary said to the others on the committee.

3. carolina exclaimed excitedly, "i was elected class president!"

4. "feed the dog right now!" tom demanded.

5. mrs. franklin announced to the class, "our field trip is tomorrow, so please be at the school at 8:00."